~A BINGO BOOK~

Figurative Language BingoBook

COMPLETE BINGO GAME IN A BOOK

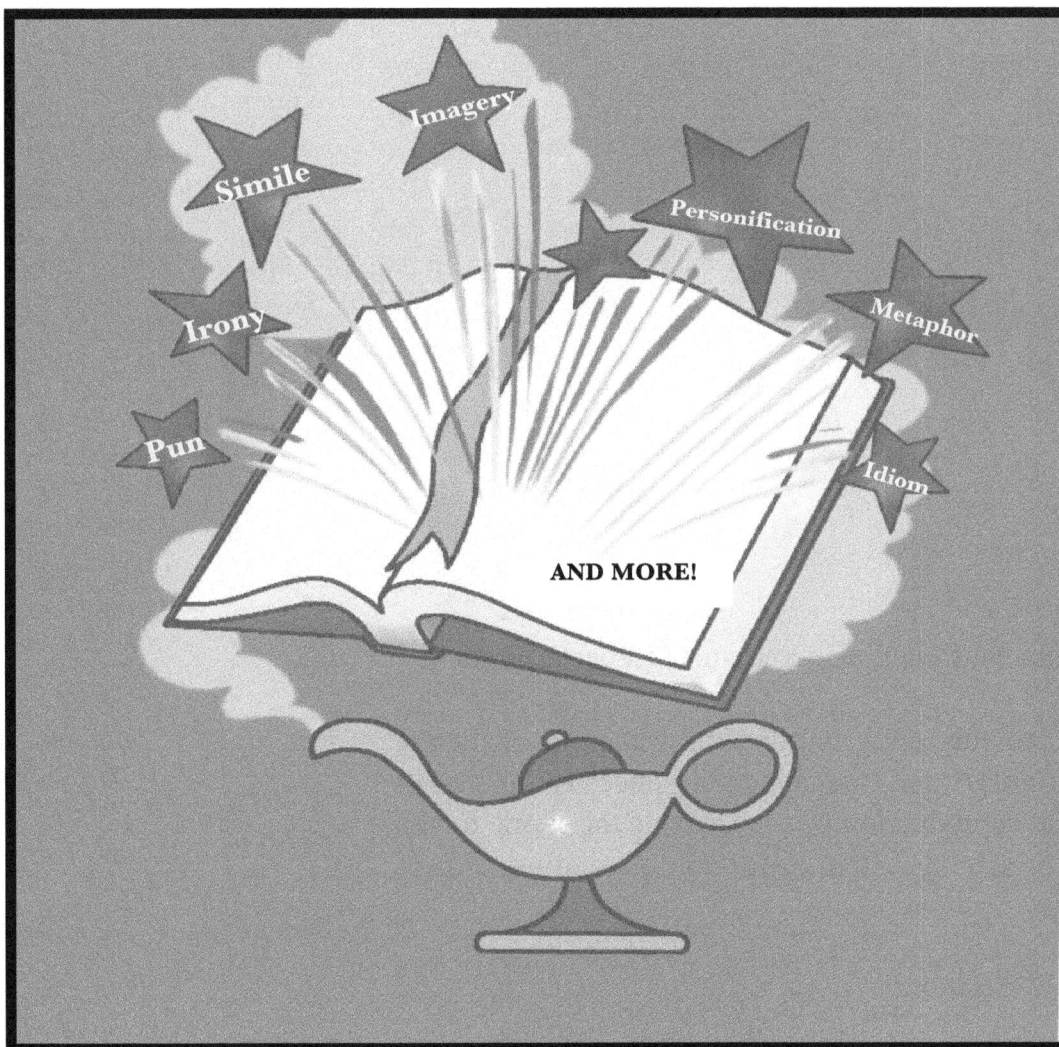

Written by Rebecca Stark
Educational Books 'n' Bingo

ISBN 978-0-87386-422-0

Educational Books 'n' Bingo

Printed in the U.S.A.

FIGURATIVE LANGUAGE BINGO
Directions

INCLUDED:

List of Terms

Templates for Additional Terms and Clues

2 Clues per Term

30 Unique Bingo Cards

Markers

1. **Either cut apart the book or make copies of ALL the sheets. You might want to make an extra copy of the clue sheets to use for introduction and review. Keep the sheets in an envelope for easy reuse.**

2. Cut apart the call cards with terms and clues.

3. Pass out one bingo card per student. There are enough for a class of 30.

4. Pass out markers. You may cut apart the markers included in this book or use any other small items of your choice.

5. Decide whether or not you will require the entire card to be filled. Requiring the entire card to be filled provides a better review. However, if you have a short time to fill, you may prefer to have them do the just the border or some other format. Tell the class before you begin what is required.

6. There are 50 topics. Read the list before you begin. If there are any topics that have not been covered in class, you may want to read to the students the topic and clues before you begin.

7. There is a blank space in the middle of each card. You can instruct the students to use it as a free space or you can write in answers to cover topics not included. Of course, in this case you would create your own clues. (Templates provided.)

8. Shuffle the cards and place them in a pile. Two or three clues are provided for each topic. If you plan to play the game with the same group more than once, you might want to choose a different clue for each game. If not, you may choose to use more than one clue.

9. Be sure to keep the cards you have used for the present game in a separate pile. When a student calls, "Bingo," he or she will have to verify that the correct answers are on his or her card AND that the markers were placed in response to the proper questions. Pull out the cards that are on the student's card keeping them in the order they were used in the game. Read each clue as it was given and ask the student to identify the correct answer from his or her card.

10. If the student has the correct answers on the card AND has shown that they were marked in response to the *correct questions,* then that student is the winner and the game is over. If the student does not have the correct answers on the card OR he or she marked the answers in response to *the wrong questions,* then the game continues until there is a proper winner.

11. If you want to play again, reshuffle the cards and begin again.

Have Fun!

TERMS

ALLEGORY	LITOTE
ALLITERATION	METAPHOR
ALLUSION	METONYMY
ANAPHORA	MOOD
ANASTROPHE	ONOMATOPOEIA
ANTHROPOMORPHISM	OXYMORON
ANTITHESIS	PARADOX
APOSTROPHE	PERSONIFICATION
ASSONANCE	POINT OF VIEW
CHARACTERIZATION	PORTMANTEAU WORDS
CLICHÉS	PUN
CONNOTATION	RHETORICAL QUESTION
DIALECT	SARCASM
DIALOGUE	SATIRE
EPILOGUE	SIMILE
EUPHEMISM	SPOONERISMS
FIGURATIVE LANGUAGE	STEREOTYPE
FLASHBACK	STYLE
FOIL	SUSPENSE
FORESHADOWING	SYMBOLISM
GENRE	SYNECHDOCHE
HYPERBOLE	THEME
IDIOM	TONE
IMAGERY	UNDERSTATEMENT
IRONY	ZEUGMA

Clues for Additional Terms

Write three clues for each of your additional terms.

_____ 1. 2. 3.	_____ 1. 2. 3.
_____ 1. 2. 3.	_____ 1. 2. 3.
_____ 1. 2. 3.	_____ 1. 2. 3.

Additional Terms

Choose as many additional terms as you would like and write them in the squares. Repeat each as desired.
Cut out the squares and randomly distribute them to the class.
Instruct the students to place their square on the center space of their card.

Figurative Language Bingo

Allegory

1. It is a story with two meanings, a literal meaning and a symbolic meaning.
2. Like a symbol, it conveys abstract ideas to get a point across; however, it differs from a symbol in that it is a complete narrative.
3. Dante's *Inferno* is an example of this extended metaphor.

Alliteration

1. It is the repetition of consonant sounds.
2. The repeated consonant in this sound pattern usually comes at the beginning of words.
3. "While I **n**odded, **n**early **n**apping" from Poe's *The Raven* is an example of this.

Allusion

1. This is a reference in a literary work to something outside of the work.
2. If you referred to someone as a Scrooge, you would be using this literary device.
3. In *Romeo and Juliet,* Montague's reference to Aurora, the Roman goddess of the dawn, is an example of this.

Anaphora

1. In rhetoric it is the repetition of the a word or set of words in successive sentences, clauses, or phrases.
2. *A Tale of Two Cities* starts out, "It was the best of times, it was the worst of times...." In this passage the repetition of "it was" is an example of this rhetorical device.
3. An example is in *Night,* by Elie Wiesel. Seven sentences in a row begin, "Never shall I forget."

Anastrophe

1. It is the inversion of the normal word order for emphasis.
2. "To war went he" is an example.
3. In George Lucas's *Star Question,* Yoda uses this rhetorical device. An example is "Ready are you?"

Anthropomorphism

1. It is the portraying of animals or inanimate objects as people.
2. Winnie the Pooh, Tigger and Piglet and other characters in children's books are examples of this device.
3. The mice and rats in *The Rats of NIMH*, by Robert C. O'Brien, are examples of this device.

Antithesis

1. It is the rhetorical contrast of ideas by means of parallel constructions.
2. An example of this rhetorical device is Neil Armstrong's statement "One small step for man, one giant leap for mankind."
3. In *Julius Caesar*, by Shakespeare, Brutus's statement "Not that I loved Caesar less, but that I loved Rome more" is an example.

Apostrophe

1. It is when someone not there or something not human is addressed as if alive and present.
2. An example of this is found in the first line of "Bright Star," by John Keats: "Bright star, would I were stedfast (sic) as thou art—."
3. This device is usually used when a speaker breaks off and addresses someone or something not there.

Assonance

1. It is the repetition of vowel sounds within neighboring words.
2. An example of this poetic device can be found in Poe's "The Bells." An example is the phrase "Fr**o**m the m**o**lten-g**o**lden n**o**tes."
3. Another example of this device from "The Bells," by Edgar Allan Poe, is this line: "Hear the m**e**llow w**e**dding-b**e**lls."

Figurative Language Bingo

Characterization

1. It is the method used by an author to develop a character.
2. It is how the author conveys to the readers a character's personality, values, physical attributes, and other traits.
3. It refers to the literary techniques that writers use to develop a character.

Clichés	**Connotation**
1. They are overused phrases or expressions. 2. The idiom "it's raining cats and dogs" is one. 3. Because these are used so often, they are often ineffective.	1. It is the associated meaning of a word or a phrase. 2. An antonym is *denotation,* or the clearly expressed meaning of a word or phrase. 3. The word *slender* has a positive one for most people; the word *skinny* has a negative one for most.
Dialect	**Dialogue**
1. It is language that is characteristic of a particular region or group. 2. This excerpt from *Treasure Island,* by Stevenson, is an example of it: "This is a handy cove, and a pleasant sittyated grog-shop." 3. This excerpt from *The Adventures of Tom Sawyer,* by Twain, is an example of it: "Tom, it was middling warm in school, warn't it?"	1. It is the spoken words between characters in a literary work. 2. It is the conversation between characters in a drama or narrative. 3. This gives a literary work a more conversational flow.
Epilogue	**Euphemism**
1. It is a piece of writing at the end of a literary work. 2. In a play, this may be used to summarize or comment on the main action. 3. Its antonym is *prologue.*	1. It is the substitution of a less explicit term for an offensive, explicit term. 2. Saying a person "passed away" rather than "died" is an example of this. 3. Saying an animal is being "put to sleep" is one.
Figurative Language	**Flashback**
1. In this type of language the words and phrases go beyond their literal meanings. 2. Simile, metaphor and personification are three common types of this kind of language. 3. Idioms are a form of this type of language.	1. This narrative technique interrupts the chronological sequence of events to describe past events. 2. This technique can help the reader understand what is going on in the present by explaining what happened in the past. 3. This telling about past events can give the reader clues about a character's motivation.
Foil	**Foreshadowing**
1. It is a character who contrasts with another character, usually the protagonist. 2. The practical Sancho Panza is one; he is contrasted with the idealistic Don Quixote. 3. Dr. Watson is one; he is contrasted with Sherlock Holmes.	1. This refers to when an author drops hints about things that will occur later in the story. 2. Shakespeare used this technique in *Julius Caesar* when the soothsayer warns Caesar to beware the Ides of March. 3. Shakespeare used this technique in *Romeo and Juliet* when the characters say that they would rather die than live apart.

Figurative Language Bingo

© **Barbara M Peller**

Genre (Literary) 1. It is a category of literature. 2. Science fiction, historical fiction and mystery are three. 3. The three basic literary ones are poetry, drama, and prose.	**Hyperbole** 1. This figure of speech is an exaggeration. 2. If your friend says to you, "I tried to call you a million times," it is likely an example of this. 3. Although the following might be thought of as a simile, it is this figure of speech: "He is as tall as a giraffe."
Idiom 1. This type of Figurative involves a term or phrase whose meaning cannot be deduced from their literal definitions. 2. A common one is "a little bird told me." 3. Another common one is "to put all your eggs in one basket."	**Imagery** 1. This refers to the use of descriptive language that appeal to the readers' senses. 2. It is language that stimulates one or more of the senses: hearing, taste, touch, smell, or sight. 3. The following phrases in *The Call of the Wild,* by Jack London, exemplify ___: **big** house; **sun-kissed**…Valley; **wide, cool** veranda; **green** pastures; and kept **cool** in the **hot** afternoon.
Irony 1. It refers to how something is not as it seems. There are several types, including verbal, dramatic and situational. 2. Verbal ___ is the use of words to express something other than and usually the opposite of the literal meaning. Sarcasm is an example. 3. Situational ___ is an outcome contrary to what was or might have been expected.	**Litote** 1. This literary device is the use of understatement for emphasis by denying the opposite of the thing being affirmed. 2. An example of this literary device is saying, "It's not the best movie I ever saw" to mean it was not a good movie. 3. An example of this ___ is saying, "This dessert isn't bad" to mean the dessert is good.
Metaphor 1. This is a comparison between two unlike things without the use of *like* or *as.* 2. This figure of speech says something *is* something else when in reality it is not. 3. An example of this figure of speech is found in *Little Women,* by Louisa May Alcott, when Jo calls Amy "a little goose."	**Metonymy** 1. ___ refers to the substitution of one term with another that is loosely associated with that term. 2. "The pen is mightier than the sword" is one. The word *pen* has been substituted for "written words that express thoughts" and the word *sword* has been substituted for "military action." 3. The use of the term "the Crown" to represent a king or queen is an example of this.
Mood 1. This literary element is the feeling the author creates for the readers. 2. It is the atmosphere or emotional condition created by the work. 3. This literary element is the general feeling the reader gets from reading the work.	**Onomatopoeia** 1. This refers to the use of words that sound like the sounds they describe. 2. Use of words such as *buzz* and *hiss* are examples of this. 3. In "The Bells" Poe uses this device to let us hear the different kinds of bells: "tinkling" sleigh bells, "clanging" fire bells, "chiming" wedding bells and so on.

Figurative Language Bingo

© **Barbara M Peller**

Oxymoron	**Paradox**
1. It is a figure of speech that combines two usually contradictory terms. 2. An example of this figure of speech is "deafening silence." 3. In Shakespeare's *Romeo and Juliet,* "Parting is such sweet sorrow" contains one.	1. It is an assertion that seems to make no sense, but that has some truth in it on closer examination. 2. It is a statement that seems contradictory but reveals a truth. 3. G.K. Chesterton's statement that "spies do not look like spies" is an example of rhetorical ___.
Personification	**Point of View**
1. It is the bestowing of human qualities on inanimate objects, ideas and animals. 2. An example of ___ is "the sun peeped into the window." 3. This example of this form of figurative language is from *Oliver Twist,* by Dickens: "There are smiling fields and waving trees."	1. It is the perspective from which a story is told. 2. If a story is told from a first-person ___, one of the characters is telling the story. 3. If a story is told from a third-person ___, none of the characters is telling the story.
Portmanteau Words	**Pun**
1. These are sometimes called blended words. 2. Some examples of ___ are *brunch* and *motel.* 3. Lewis Carroll used them and coined the word. In *Through the Looking Glass* Humpty Dumpty explains to Alice that "*slithy* means lithe and slimy."	1. This form of figurative language uses words that sound the same but have different meanings to create a humorous or rhetorical effect. 2. It is a humorous play on words which are similar in sound but different in meaning. 3. This excerpt from *Charlie & The Chocolate Factory*, by Dahl, is one: "A poached egg isn't a poached egg unless it's been stolen from the woods…."
Rhetorical Question	**Sarcasm**
1. This figure of speech is a question that is posed for a desired effect without the expectation of a reply. 2. If someone tells you something surprising and you reply, "You're kidding!" you're likely using this. 3. If a mother says to her child, "How many times do I have to tell you to pick up your things?" she is using this figure of speech.	1. It is a form of verbal irony in which a person says the opposite of what he or she means. 2. *In Crispin, the Cross of Lead,* by Avi, Bear uses this form of irony in response to Crispin's short answers: "You have a gifted way of speech." 3. It may be described as verbal irony that is intended to insult or ridicule.
Satire	**Simile**
1. It is a literary work that pokes fun at individual or societal weaknesses. 2. Although this literary genre is usually meant to be funny, its main purpose is to attack something of which the author disapproves. 3. In this genre the author uses wit and humor to poke fun at something and show disapproval.	1. This is a comparison between two unlike things using the words *like* or as. 2. A ___ says something is *like* something else although the two are quite different. 3. In *The Lost World,* Conan Doyle used this form of figurative language to describe the male pterodactyls: "They sat like gigantic old women, wrapped in…shawls."

Figurative Language Bingo

Spoonerisms	**Stereotype**
1. They are words or phrases in which letters or syllables get swapped. 2. This transposition of initial or other sounds of words is usually accidental but may also be intentionally done for effect. 3. They were named after an English clergyman. One of the things he supposedly said was "Is the bean dizzy?" instead of "Is the dean busy?"	1. It is a generalization about a group of people. 2. It is the attributing of a defined set of characteristics to a group of people. 3. It is a positive or negative set of beliefs regarding the characteristics of a group of people.
Style	**Suspense**
1. It refers to an author's manner of writing, including grammar, vocabulary, the use of figurative language and other factors. 2. Some elements of literary ___ include sentence structure, use of dialogue, vocabulary, point of view, character development, and tone. 3. Some general ones are straightforward, descriptive, scientific, and fanciful.	1. It is the quality that makes readers wonder what will happen next. 2. It is apprehension about what will happen. 3. Mysteries usually have this quality.
Symbolism	**Synechdoche**
1. It is the use of an object, character or idea to represent something else. 2. The use of coffee to represent Jethro's coming of age in *Across Five Aprils,* by Irene Hunt, is an example of this. 3. The use of the mockingbird to represent innocence in *To Kill a Mockingbird,* by Harper Lee, is an example of this.	1. Using the word *hands* to represent those aboard the ship in "All hands on deck" is an example of ___. 2. Using the USA to stand for the athletes in "The USA won ten gold medals" is an example. 3. Although ___ is similar to metonymy, metonymy uses something more loosely associated with the concept as a replacement.
Theme	**Tone**
1. It is the main idea of a literary work; the idea the author wants to convey. 2. The importance of family is a common one. 3. Good versus evil is a common one.	1. This literary element is the author's attitude toward the writing. 2. It may be serious, humorous, sarcastic, ironic, satirical, tongue-in-cheek, solemn, or objective. 3. Many confuse this with mood, but this is the writer's attitude toward what he or she is writing and mood is the feeling the reader gets when reading it.
Understatement	**Zeugma**
1. This is the stating of something less strongly than the facts seem to warrant. 2. "It's just a little breeze" to describe a hurricane would be an example. 3. A litote is a form of this.	1. It is the use of a verb to modify or govern two or more words although it has a different sense for each or is appropriate for only one. 2. The use of *take* in this excerpt from Alexander Pope's *The Rape of the Lock* is an example: "Dost sometimes counsel take—and sometimes tea." 3. This excerpt from Dickens' *The Pickwick* is one: "Mr. Pickwick took his hat and his leave."

Figurative Language Bingo

Figurative Language Bingo

Simile	Allegory	Anaphora	Idiom	Characterization
Anthropomorphism	Alliteration	Suspense	Paradox	Understatement
Theme	Synechdoche		Point of View	Tone
Zeugma	Euphemism	Style	Mood	Personification
Portmanteau Words	Foil	Hyperbole	Symbolism	Metaphor

Figurative Language Bingo

Zeugma	Theme	Metonymy	Spoonerisms	Genre
Personification	Dialogue	Apostrophe	Euphemism	Onomatopoeia
Connotation	Foil		Flashback	Style
Pun	Satire	Synechdoche	Sarcasm	Characterization
Understatement	Suspense	Hyperbole	Anthropomorphism	Symbolism

Figurative Language Bingo: Card No. 2

Figurative Language Bingo

Foil	Style	Dialogue	Mood	Theme
Personification	Alliteration	Assonance	Allegory	Irony
Euphemism	Suspense		Onomatopoeia	Allusion
Synechdoche	Connotation	Portmanteau Words	Pun	Metonymy
Symbolism	Anthropomorphism	Hyperbole	Sarcasm	Genre

Figurative Language Bingo

Synechdoche	Onomatopoeia	Anaphora	Anthropomorphism	Genre
Litote	Antithesis	Allegory	Spoonerisms	Theme
Point of View	Pun		Metaphor	Idiom
Style	Figurative Language	Suspense	Hyperbole	Apostrophe
Clichés	Understatement	Anastrophe	Symbolism	Tone

Figurative Language Bingo

Understatement	Characterization	Euphemism	Apostrophe	Anthropomorphism
Litote	Style	Assonance	Flashback	Alliteration
Anaphora	Tone		Paradox	Imagery
Metaphor	Genre	Simile	Sarcasm	Dialect
Dialogue	Hyperbole	Theme	Synechdoche	Point of View

Figurative Language Bingo: Card No. 5

Figurative Language Bingo

Allusion	Onomatopoeia	Metonymy	Genre	Tone
Mood	Euphemism	Dialect	Allegory	Theme
Spoonerisms	Clichés		Antithesis	Flashback
Hyperbole	Portmanteau Words	Sarcasm	Anastrophe	Anaphora
Personification	Apostrophe	Simile	Point of View	Figurative Language

Figurative Language Bingo

Simile	Onomatopoeia	Imagery	Style	Dialogue
Personification	Genre	Foil	Alliteration	Litote
Metonymy	Idiom		Flashback	Antithesis
Synechdoche	Pun	Assonance	Zeugma	Connotation
Hyperbole	Anthropomorphism	Sarcasm	Anastrophe	Allusion

Figurative Language Bingo

Point of View	Onomatopoeia	Epilogue	Mood	Antithesis
Litote	Anaphora	Spoonerisms	Tone	Apostrophe
Figurative Language	Rhetorical Question		Genre	Characterization
Symbolism	Synechdoche	Zeugma	Clichés	Pun
Suspense	Hyperbole	Anastrophe	Euphemism	Personification

© **Barbara M Peller**

Figurative Language Bingo

Flashback	Dialogue	Foil	Figurative Language	Anthropomorphism
Clichés	Genre	Point of View	Euphemism	Onomatopoeia
Irony	Simile		Alliteration	Epilogue
Dialect	Characterization	Portmanteau Words	Paradox	Imagery
Pun	Sarcasm	Assonance	Zeugma	Metaphor

Figurative Language Bingo

Zeugma	Mood	Antithesis	Spoonerisms	Figurative Language
Tone	Apostrophe	Allegory	Alliteration	Genre
Rhetorical Question	Onomatopoeia		Idiom	Connotation
Portmanteau Words	Metaphor	Dialect	Sarcasm	Irony
Assonance	Personification	Metonymy	Understatement	Point of View

Figurative Language Bingo

Allusion	Onomatopoeia	Euphemism	Dialect	Personification
Epilogue	Irony	Paradox	Flashback	Allegory
Litote	Genre		Metonymy	Foil
Assonance	Theme	Sarcasm	Anthropomorphism	Zeugma
Clichés	Hyperbole	Simile	Anastrophe	Dialogue

© Barbara M Peller

Figurative Language Bingo

Dialogue	Characterization	Irony	Mood	Flashback
Foil	Personification	Anaphora	Anastrophe	Alliteration
Simile	Imagery		Tone	Spoonerisms
Hyperbole	Pun	Genre	Zeugma	Litote
Onomatopoeia	Epilogue	Rhetorical Question	Clichés	Apostrophe

Figurative Language Bingo

Dialect	Characterization	Allusion	Irony	Tone
Anaphora	Epilogue	Genre	Flashback	Connotation
Mood	Apostrophe		Foil	Imagery
Point of View	Sarcasm	Antithesis	Rhetorical Question	Zeugma
Hyperbole	Metaphor	Anastrophe	Simile	Paradox

Figurative Language Bingo: Card No. 13

Figurative Language Bingo

Anthropomorphism	Genre	Euphemism	Flashback	Clichés
Apostrophe	Simile	Irony	Alliteration	Onomatopoeia
Dialect	Idiom		Metonymy	Assonance
Metaphor	Sarcasm	Rhetorical Question	Antithesis	Allusion
Hyperbole	Spoonerisms	Connotation	Personification	Point of View

Figurative Language Bingo

Paradox	Flashback	Euphemism	Dialogue	Mood
Allusion	Metonymy	Allegory	Anaphora	Clichés
Tone	Simile		Theme	Onomatopoeia
Hyperbole	Irony	Epilogue	Sarcasm	Dialect
Personification	Pun	Anastrophe	Figurative Language	Foil

Figurative Language Bingo

Antithesis	Irony	Epilogue	Figurative Language	Satire
Spoonerisms	Connotation	Imagery	Litote	Idiom
Dialect	Characterization		Tone	Foil
Synechdoche	Apostrophe	Hyperbole	Paradox	Zeugma
Clichés	Stereotype	Anastrophe	Pun	Onomatopoeia

Figurative Language Bingo

Assonance	Oxymoron	Foreshadowing	Irony	Anthropomorphism
Paradox	Clichés	Sarcasm	Idiom	Imagery
Flashback	Point of View		Stereotype	Epilogue
Metaphor	Personification	Zeugma	Euphemism	Connotation
Portmanteau Words	Dialect	Dialogue	Mood	Characterization

Figurative Language Bingo: Card No. 17

Figurative Language Bingo

Figurative Language	Rhetorical Question	Apostrophe	Dialect	Spoonerisms
Onomatopoeia	Assonance	Portmanteau Words	Tone	Clichés
Flashback	Connotation		Foreshadowing	Anaphora
Characterization	Allegory	Sarcasm	Zeugma	Metonymy
Stereotype	Irony	Euphemism	Oxymoron	Allusion

Figurative Language Bingo

Tone	Allusion	Irony	Epilogue	Zeugma
Paradox	Mood	Onomatopoeia	Dialogue	Idiom
Oxymoron	Anthropomorphism		Alliteration	Theme
Metonymy	Stereotype	Portmanteau Words	Pun	Foreshadowing
Anaphora	Satire	Personification	Point of View	Anastrophe

© **Barbara M Peller**

Figurative Language Bingo

Rhetorical Question	Oxymoron	Mood	Irony	Anastrophe
Apostrophe	Foil	Litote	Portmanteau Words	Spoonerisms
Characterization	Imagery		Synechdoche	Allegory
Understatement	Suspense	Symbolism	Pun	Stereotype
Style	Point of View	Satire	Zeugma	Foreshadowing

Figurative Language Bingo

Paradox	Allusion	Litote	Irony	Understatement
Characterization	Foreshadowing	Antithesis	Epilogue	Simile
Connotation	Personification		Oxymoron	Euphemism
Portmanteau Words	Dialogue	Stereotype	Metaphor	Point of View
Synechdoche	Satire	Anastrophe	Assonance	Pun

Figurative Language Bingo: Card No. 21

Figurative Language Bingo

Figurative Language	Metonymy	Foreshadowing	Anaphora	Dialect
Spoonerisms	Mood	Theme	Epilogue	Alliteration
Apostrophe	Idiom		Simile	Imagery
Stereotype	Metaphor	Pun	Allegory	Anthropomorphism
Satire	Assonance	Oxymoron	Connotation	Litote

Figurative Language Bingo: Card No. 22

Figurative Language Bingo

Antithesis	Oxymoron	Dialogue	Anaphora	Anastrophe
Allusion	Rhetorical Question	Personification	Paradox	Allegory
Metonymy	Dialect		Symbolism	Simile
Connotation	Satire	Stereotype	Assonance	Pun
Understatement	Suspense	Point of View	Portmanteau Words	Foreshadowing

Figurative Language Bingo

Antithesis	Rhetorical Question	Anthropomorphism	Oxymoron	Epilogue
Foreshadowing	Anastrophe	Litote	Spoonerisms	Simile
Imagery	Figurative Language		Dialect	Connotation
Understatement	Symbolism	Stereotype	Assonance	Characterization
Style	Synechdoche	Satire	Mood	Suspense

Figurative Language Bingo

Synechdoche	Litote	Oxymoron	Euphemism	Foreshadowing
Allegory	Characterization	Paradox	Antithesis	Alliteration
Metaphor	Epilogue		Symbolism	Stereotype
Theme	Understatement	Suspense	Satire	Idiom
Anastrophe	Anthropomorphism	Apostrophe	Clichés	Style

Figurative Language Bingo

Foreshadowing	Oxymoron	Metonymy	Spoonerisms	Figurative Language
Portmanteau Words	Mood	Epilogue	Rhetorical Question	Antithesis
Metaphor	Symbolism		Idiom	Synechdoche
Assonance	Anaphora	Understatement	Satire	Stereotype
Imagery	Clichés	Euphemism	Suspense	Style

© **Barbara M Peller**

Figurative Language Bingo

Metonymy	Apostrophe	Oxymoron	Rhetorical Question	Foil
Understatement	Symbolism	Paradox	Stereotype	Alliteration
Sarcasm	Suspense		Satire	Synechdoche
Figurative Language	Allusion	Litote	Style	Allegory
Clichés	Idiom	Foreshadowing	Theme	Imagery

© **Barbara M Peller**

Figurative Language Bingo

Figurative Language	Rhetorical Question	Theme	Oxymoron	Antithesis
Foil	Foreshadowing	Symbolism	Spoonerisms	Idiom
Suspense	Connotation		Imagery	Portmanteau Words
Zeugma	Pun	Personification	Satire	Stereotype
Anaphora	Flashback	Clichés	Style	Understatement

Figurative Language Bingo

Foreshadowing	Rhetorical Question	Figurative Language	Paradox	Flashback
Simile	Portmanteau Words	Litote	Imagery	Theme
Metaphor	Symbolism		Alliteration	Oxymoron
Foil	Understatement	Genre	Satire	Stereotype
Antithesis	Epilogue	Style	Allusion	Suspense

Figurative Language Bingo

Anthropomorphism	Oxymoron	Spoonerisms	Flashback	Stereotype
Allegory	Rhetorical Question	Metonymy	Idiom	Alliteration
Metaphor	Dialect		Imagery	Litote
Style	Allusion	Anaphora	Satire	Symbolism
Understatement	Tone	Suspense	Foreshadowing	Theme

Figurative Language Bingo: Card No. 30